BEST ENFJ EVER

Leverage Your Strengths to Achieve Success, Wealth & Happiness

THE SECRET ACTION PLAN

CHRIS FOX

BEST ENFJ EVER. First paperback edition, November 2023.

Published by Attraxio Company Limited, Thailand.

ISBN – Paperback: 978-9-693-89259-8
An e-book version is available at ChrisFox.com.

Check out the complementary tools and resources
available exclusively at **chrisfox.com/enfj-book-tools**

Table of Contents

Contents

BEST ENFJ EVER

Dedication

To my mother,

who has been a beacon of light and strength in my life. Your unwavering support and love have shaped me, and this book stands as a testament to all you've taught me.

"*We can only be said to be alive in those moments when our hearts are conscious of our treasures.*"
—*Thornton Wilder*

Acknowledgments

I want to express my deepest gratitude to the special people who have supported me throughout this book-writing journey and those new friends who continue to inspire me daily.

My cherished partner, Wirantorn, for helping me distill my thoughts into a title that says it all. Your patience and understanding during my writing sessions and helping me remember to enjoy life outside of work have meant the world to me.

Dirk Weeber Arayatumsopon, PhD, your feedback, rigorous thought processes, and ENFJ kinship enriched both the book and my life.

Ronnie Chia, your friendship and kindheartedness know no bounds, nor does your mastery in harmonizing life's vibrations. You uniquely understand how the energy we emit impacts our environment and vice versa. I am grateful you share that healing wisdom with the world.

Vishen Lakhiani, your groundbreaking work in personal development through Mindvalley has been a guiding light. Your teachings, especially the Silva Ultramind System, have expanded my understanding of human capabilities.

"*In helping others, we shall help ourselves,
for whatever good we give out completes the circle
and comes back to us.*"
—*Flora Edwards*

Acknowledgments

Richard Ker, your unique storytelling style in innovation and entrepreneurship is ever more captivating and empowering in our world of fleeting focus. Your approach to sharing knowledge is uplifting to ENFJs like me.

Vincent Vandeputte and Dirk Theuns, your strength of character to stand up for what is right and just in a time of great adversity, and all of it with a positive and humorous undertone, has had a profound impact on me. You have set the bar high for authentic leadership, and for that, you have my unyielding admiration.

Thank you also to the ENFJs who have shared their struggles and techniques to overcome them. None of this would have been possible without you.

Lastly, I am thankful for the many other friends, mentors, colleagues, and clients who have motivated, challenged, and supported me throughout my life and career. You know who you are, and I am grateful for each of you.

Thank you!
Chris Fox

"Find out what you like doing best and get someone to pay you for doing it."
—*Katharine Whitehorn*

Introduction

Imagine waking up each morning to a life where your work doesn't just pay the bills but deeply fulfills you, fueling your soul and dreams. Sounds like a fantasy? It's your potential reality, and as an ENFJ, it's much closer than you think! Let me take you on a journey that may echo some of your own experiences.

In the heart of my home country, I found my first love—radio. I wasn't spinning records, though, but I was part of nearly every management aspect. From music selection, writing copy, and scheduling talents to the technical revolution my geeky self had envisioned. Sick of the sounds of crackling records and warbling tapes, we became the first stations to play all music from hard disks, long before MP3 was a thing! The thrill was immediate; I could drive through the city and hear our programming emanate from car radios and shop windows. It was a direct line to people's lives—instant feedback—and I was hooked!

But life, as it often does, threw a curveball, and the media landscape turned into a political battleground. If you didn't pick a political side, you wouldn't survive. The joy began to wane, but another door was opening. The internet (called Fidonet at the time, woof!) was this new, wild frontier, and I jumped in headfirst. After learning web design and turning it into a business, I spotted a unique opportunity. It was an era before *Facebook, YouTube,* and

"We must be willing to let go of the life we planned so as to have the life that is waiting for us."
—Joseph Campbell

WhatsApp, and *Yahoo!* was the closest to a search engine. So, I partnered with a developer and built a web directory that quickly became one of the country's most famous sites. Helping millions of users find precisely what they want each month, hundreds of millions of visits over the years, *and* allowing me to work from anywhere was intoxicating! It also led me to a decision that would change my life.

I moved to Thailand, a place so totally different yet so welcoming. The people were warm, the culture rich; even the rain felt kinder! Knowing not a soul when I arrived, my daily goal was building my social circle. I have some of the fondest memories of that time; still, I wish I had done things very differently!

You see, I had financial freedom, but I lacked a financial mentor. *Big mistake!* And then the storm hit! The pan-European ad agency that sold ads on the site to A-listers like BMW and Coca-Cola was taken over, and within two months, I lost 75% of my monthly revenue. Other sites didn't fare any better, either. Lesson: don't put all your eggs in one basket! I had started losing affinity with my home country through my extended stay in Asia, though, so I sold off the site years later.

Meanwhile, a chance encounter led me into the world of coaching. I had always been interested in personal development, and the communication aspect was also evident. So, after a few days of intensive soul-searching with like-minded souls, this still shy person felt his feet carry him to the front of a stage at a Singapore event to declare in front of nearly a thousand others his desire to uplift people. There was no turning back!

And so I started helping people communicate better with their loved ones, be their best possible selves, reach new heights, or achieve breakthroughs in their business. I loved hearing their stories about how, sometimes, even just a social media post had

*"The more you know yourself,
the more you forgive yourself."*
—*Confucius*

changed their lives. **Note:** You will never even be aware of most of your impact on people's lives.

One of the friends I made in Singapore later invited me to join a network marketing company. I had never heard of this type of business, but I would be able to hone my coaching skills further, so I agreed. Despite the success of the first few years, it turned disastrous. Only later did I fully understand why that career was a total mismatch, and I briefly discuss it in *Chapter Four* of this book.

The worst thing that happened at the time was that some of my closest friends' scathing critiques totally and utterly obliterated my self-confidence and self-worth. It was so bad that I questioned *all* of my abilities to the point where I sometimes coached people for free to feel even the tiniest bit useful!

I was still coaching and, apparently, pretty good at it, with only happy clients, but the critiques directed at me earlier prevented me from seeing any of it. Each day, **I was fueling other people's success but sacrificing my own.**

It was a bad situation that lasted for *years*, with the ensuing perfectionism aggravating it. I was building new projects and starting new ventures. Some paid off; some didn't, but the truth is I felt lifeless inside. My passion was gone. All the criticism I had ever received kept playing in my head non-stop until my diminished self-worth turned into a full-blown minority complex! I was in a tailspin. It wouldn't end well, and *I knew it!* Nobody was coming to save me. *It had to be me!*

That's when I began writing this guide, initially as a lifeline for myself. I wanted to understand and put a stop to my self-sabotage, discover my true purpose, and unlock the potential that *I knew* I had in me.

"*The pessimist complains about the wind.*
The optimist expects it to change.
The leader adjusts the sails."
—*John Maxwell*

In this storm, I found my compass, my ENFJ personality type—a blessing when understood and utilized, yet an outright curse when ignored. Suddenly, I understood why radio and the internet had felt so fulfilling—they aligned with my ENFJ strengths. I also saw why other ventures drained me; they were misaligned with who I was. I became fascinated, read up on reports, consulted with fellow ENFJs about their experiences, and documented my own. I wanted to experience daily joy again and a profound sense of accomplishment before bed.

It took me a lot of time—that dreaded perfectionism again—but it was the only way to achieve the breakthrough I needed. Soon, I became **more purposeful in my decision-making** and started once again attracting those lucky "coincidences" that have pulled me toward my dreams and a more fulfilled life ever since. Armed with this newfound wisdom, I felt compelled to share it.

Luckily, you don't have to take a multi-year sabbatical to discover your true self like I did. Nor should you keep crashing into walls or hit rock bottom before you realize something needs to change!

So, if you've ever felt lost, stuck, or unfulfilled, **this book is your shortcut to clarity**, a roadmap to a fulfilling life without the many detours and dead-ends.

This isn't a collection of endless stories or boring explanations. **It's a book designed for action**, with concise, bullet-point guidance, tools, and resources to get you unstuck and moving forward.

We won't dwell on "why things happened." Instead, we'll focus on the "what" and "how." We will uncover your core values and motivations, explore compatible career paths, and navigate around the pitfalls that have tripped you up in the past.

Remember, you're not just reading a book; you're *actively reshaping your future.*

"Your future depends on what you do today."
—*Mahatma Gandhi*

So, are you ready to stop dreaming?
Are you ready to start living?
Are you ready to become your best ENFJ version ever?
Your future is waiting, and it looks incredible!
Let's get started!

"Don't let someone else's opinion of you become your reality."
—Les Brown

How This Book Will Help You

As an ENFJ, our multifaceted talents and interests can sometimes lead to **decision paralysis**—fear of choosing the wrong path.

It's a common dilemma driven by various factors:

- Perhaps you've experienced setbacks in roles that didn't suit you, dealt with challenging personalities, or approached great opportunities with simply the wrong mindset.

- Your self-confidence might have taken a hit, making it seem like there are no viable career options that would ever lead to a happy life!

- You might be yearning for a fresh start in an entirely new field, or your aspirations are reaching for the stars, but you lack guidance on making them a reality.

- Your diverse interests may pull you in multiple directions, leaving you torn between your passions.

- External pressures, such as financial obligations, family expectations, or societal norms, could be urging you to make a quick decision, but you simply don't know how!

You'll be able to overcome this once and for all!

"Action is the foundational key to all success."
—*Pablo Picasso*

This book is here to help you:

- Gain perfect clarity about what *truly* matters to you.

- Explore a wide array of compatible career options.

- Navigate that sea of choices and pinpoint the ideal fit, with optional midway careers along the way.

But this isn't your typical read; it's a **tool for action.** I won't define every possible quirk unique to ENFJs—plenty of reporting tools exist for that. Let's pivot straight to the actionable steps that foster a crystal-clear vision.

- **Evaluate and Rank:** You'll start by rating your strengths, weaknesses, core values, and motivational drives on a scale.

- **Answer and Reflect:** Next, questions will help you expand your self-view so it more accurately represents who you are.

- **Curate Career Choices:** You'll find the most extensive list of ENFJ-compatible careers ever printed, where you get to mark the ones that intrigue you.

- **Dodging Career Hazards:** You'll learn to spot the red flags and how to steer clear of less-optimal careers.

- **Execute Your Plan:** Finally, you'll turn these insights into a pragmatic plan for your future, identifying immediate and long-term career moves.

Ensure you have a pencil, eraser, and highlighter close at hand. These will be your companions on this journey. If you've gone the extra mile and purchased multiple copies of this book to track your progress over time, boldly use a pen and **mark your trail toward success!**

*"Become who you are. Do what only you can do.
Be the master and sculptor of yourself."*
—Friedrich Nietzsche

Chapter 1 |
Understanding Your ENFJ Traits

Are you marching to a different beat? Are you seeing the world differently than most people around you? Like you're called to serve a greater purpose in life? Maybe you're gifted with natural talents for motivating and bringing out the best in people. Or, you are able to effortlessly tune into the subtle emotions of others. If this feels like you, you're likely an ENFJ as well!

As one of the rarest of the 16 personality types in the *Myers-Briggs Type Indicator* model, a rather unique set of strengths and sensibilities set us apart. We view the world through a lens of empathy and insight. We spot possibilities that others don't and are often the first to uncover what's *really* going on.

But to make our mark in the world, we must understand ourselves to shape a career that feels right and where we can shine bright.

This chapter will help you unpack your ENFJ self. We will dig into our strengths, core values, and motivations and bring our blind spots into view to use them to our advantage!

"*The more you trust your intuition,
the more empowered you become,
the stronger you become and
the happier you become.*"
—*Gisele Bundchen*

What Is an ENFJ?

This collection of letters is the key to unlocking our fascinating personality: ENFJ stands for Extraverted, Intuitive, Feeling, and Judging, but since you're reading this book, you likely already know that, so here's only a brief overview.

In the broadest of terms, a person who is a full spectrum ENFJ exhibits the following traits at the highest level:

- **E – Extraverted**: We're people persons. We love to mingle and work with others. We make people feel at ease at a party and introduce them to one another. Making connections is easy for us, and we gain energy doing so!

- **N – Intuitive**: We're naturals at spotting patterns, noticing untapped potential, and discovering hidden meanings. Our vibrant imagination doesn't just think outside the box; often, we don't even see the box! Consequently, we're often complimented on our innovative problem-solving skills.

- **F – Feeling**: We're not just in touch with our emotions but with everyone else's too! We make decisions based on harmony and empathy, always considering how others might feel. Sometimes, even to the detriment of ourselves!

- **J – Judging**: We like things to be orderly and planned. We're decisive and focused and prefer a to-do list over winging it since we don't want to be judged poorly ourselves.

We all have these traits inside of us to some extent.

*"Satisfaction is not the absence of problems;
it's the ability to deal with them."*
—*Steve Maraboli*

Put all this together, and we get a snapshot of the ENFJ charm. You're passionate, warm, and love to help others, even more so when you can plan and create!

"How does this play out in day-to-day life? Shouldn't we all be ecstatic with joy, then? **Why do I often feel so deeply unsatisfied?***"*

Excellent point! To find out, we first need to become aware of our strengths.

It's time to get practical!

"I'm not saying I'm gonna change the world,
but I guarantee that I will spark the brain
that will change the world."
—Tupac Shakur

Strengths

We possess numerous natural talents and develop even more valuable skills over time, such as the ones below.

Are you aware of *your* most vital assets?

Using a pencil, and to the best of your abilities, **rate from highest to lowest (5 to 1; leave blank if it doesn't apply)** the **strength** of this trait in yourself. Circle it if you have only just now become aware of it. Put a (+) plus sign in front if you want to further grow this strength.

___ **Charismatic Communication:** You have a way with words that makes people sit up and listen. Whether it's connecting on a personal level through storytelling, persuading a group, or leading a discussion, you can articulate your thoughts with eloquence and clarity and have the ability to make any subject matter come alive.

___ **Diplomacy:** Even though you aren't afraid to voice your strong opinions, you respect others' right to speak their truth and look for common ground and win-win solutions.

___ **Empathy:** You excel at sensing others' emotions and providing compassion. Listening comes naturally, and you provide a safe and supportive environment, which allows you to pick up on nuances and unspoken feelings.

___ **Meaningful Relationships:** You invest time and effort in building strong bonds with people who cross your path. You're warm, likable, and good-natured in personal and professional relationships.

"Success is no accident. It is hard work, perseverance, learning, studying, sacrifice, and most of all, love of what you are doing or learning to do."
—*Pele*

___ **Motivational Skills:** You're not just enthusiastic; you're a spark that can ignite a wildfire of motivation in others. You can rally and inspire people to reach their full potential.

___ **Natural Leadership:** You're great at organizing groups and spearheading initiatives. Your charisma, vision, and leading by example draw people in, making you a magnet for followers. You have an ulterior motive, though: to turn those followers into leaders themselves!

___ **Benevolence:** You're convinced that helping and bringing people together is what the world needs and you're determined to be a part of it!

___ **Focus:** When you're committed to a goal, you have a near-superhuman capacity for sustained effort. Even when faced with seemingly insurmountable roadblocks, your determination keeps you going.

___ **Visionary Creativity:** You're an innovator at heart, able to turn abstract ideas into tangible solutions. You love to come up with fresh and unconventional approaches.

___ **Insightfulness:** Your ability to grasp the deeper meanings and underlying patterns of situations is remarkable. You see beyond the obvious, delving into the whys and hows. This gift allows you to profoundly understand people and circumstances, giving you an edge in decision-making and interpersonal relations. When ENFJs learn to balance their insightfulness, strengths, and weaknesses, they exhibit genuine wisdom.

"*The quieter you become, the more you can hear.*"
—*Ram Dass*

___ **Passion:** You brim with interests and take pleasure in pursuing hobbies. In fact, you have so many interests that it would benefit you to focus your enthusiasm and turn proficiency into mastery.

___ **Growth Mindset:** "Knowledge is power" is quite literal to you. You're immensely curious about essential matters! You're always learning. You love it and wish you could know everything. So, you become exceptional at uniquely sharing that knowledge with others.

___ **Versatility:** You transition seamlessly between tasks, roles, and environments and can handle nearly anything thrown at you.

___ **Hardworking:** You're willing to work to guarantee your success. That doesn't mean you should do all of the work yourself. Often, you're better at planning and letting others execute your intricate designs, schedules, and protocols.

___ **Reliability:** Your word is golden. Others can count on you to see your promises and responsibilities through.

Feel free to review your ratings and make any necessary adjustments if needed.

"If kids come to us from strong, healthy, functioning families, it makes our job easier. If they do not come to us from strong, healthy, functioning families, it makes our job more important."
—*Barbara Colorose*

— ENFJ Profile: Daniel

To see what these strengths look like in real life, let's hear from a high school teacher who leverages his ENFJ gifts with his students.

"My goal is to help teenagers become lifelong learners who believe in themselves. I find it kinda easy to spot each student's unique talents and potential, even when they might say they're not good at anything! You know?

It felt a lot easier growing up when I was young. There are so many distractions now. Especially with social media, where kids are constantly comparing themselves, most of them can't even find the good or uniqueness in themselves anymore.

So, every time I can give a student a gentle 'reality check,' I consider that a win. I imagine putting a star above their head like in those old-school video games! What was it again, Sonic the Hedgehog?!

I also try to make my lessons as engaging as possible. With their short attention span these days, it takes some ingenuity. I'd often say something like, 'Michael, tell me, if you'd have to put what you've learned in a 30-second video on TikTok and make it go viral, what would you do?' It's my way of imprinting essential knowledge into their heads. Turn on that habit of thinking for themselves. You know what I'm saying?

You have to roll with it, man. You can't be that old, stiff teacher dude with kids anymore. You gotta be someone they trust but who they also respect. I have to go now. I have a class coming up! Gotta put some more stars above their head so they can level up!"

"Charisma isn't about being the center of attention; it's about making others feel extraordinary in your presence."
—*Anonymous*

Daniel's charismatic and outgoing nature always brings a smile to my face. You can tell that he loves his job! It just makes him good-humored all the time, and with that, everyone around him.

He reminds me of *Gabriel Iglesias*, the comedian and actor in the 2019 sitcom *Mr. Iglesias*. If you want to hone your charisma and find ways to connect with young people, that TV series is an insightful and fun way to relax!

"One day, the people that didn't believe in you will tell everyone how they met you."
—*Johnny Depp*

How We're All Different

While we share many common traits, no two ENFJs are alike. Most of us become ENFJ as a result of our experiences, our environment, our mentors, and our tormentors.

Some areas where we might differ:

- **Social Energy:** Some are very talkative and the life of the party, while others are more reserved and selective with their social energy. Still, we all **enjoy collaborating** with passionate groups.

- **Emotional Expressiveness**: While most are open about communicating their feelings, bad experiences have taught others to be more composed. However, we all **aim for harmony** in our surroundings.

- **Idealism**: Many hold solid ideals and values. Others tend to be more pragmatic and realistic. Yet, we all strive to **make a positive difference** in the world.

- **Organization**: Some prefer strict schedules and detailed planning. Others are flexible and improvise more. But we do appreciate **some level of organization** in life.

- **Confidence:** Certain ENFJs radiate self-assurance, while another group, in private, often doubts themselves. Nonetheless, we **believe in our abilities** when we feel supported.

- **Body Image**: Some are more conscious about their body image, while others find it less important. We tend to be more public than most other personality types, so given the circumstances, we **want to look the part.**

"*If you are insecure, guess what?*
The rest of the world is, too.
Do not overestimate the competition and
underestimate yourself.
You are better than you think!"
—*Tim Ferriss*

- **Stress and Emotions**: The level of confidence also impacts how well ENFJs deal with stress and are in control of their emotions. Some are easily overwhelmed, while others are more controlled. Yet, we **can all connect on deep human levels and accomplish great things**, even under stress.

Determining our unique mix of qualities becomes straightforward when we go beyond the stereotypes and confront our blind spots and weaknesses.

*"I'm always described as 'cocksure' or 'with a swagger,'
and that bears no resemblance to
who I feel like inside."*
—*Ben Affleck*

Weaknesses & Blind Spots

Since we often are perfectionists, and our driving force in life is perpetual growth, becoming aware of our blind spots should fill us with joy.

Rate from highest to lowest (5 to 1; leave blank if it doesn't apply) the **impact** of this trait on yourself. Circle the ranking if you've only just become aware of it. Put a (-) minus sign in front if you want to reduce its impact.

___ **Taking Criticism Personally:** We quickly feel hurt as we tend to internalize negative feedback. Know that criticism and rejection are opportunities for growth, not the assaults on our character or self-worth we think they are! Feedback has the potential to enhance your effectiveness significantly!

___ **Taking on Others' Emotions:** We're empathic and often instinctively try to become the person in front of us to understand them better and give them the best possible advice. **Remember to climb back out!** Don't trade places!

___ **Impatience with Mundane Tasks:** Find ways to make them more engaging. Break them into smaller pieces or turn them into a game! We can get quite creative when we accept that completing specific tasks is needed to support our broader goals and vision. If you're in a situation where they take time and energy away from your mission, and you can outsource them, do so!

___ **Difficulty Letting Go:** As curators of knowledge, tools, and *even people*, we do well with regular decluttering. You can't put any new furniture in if the home is chock-full!

"No man will make a great leader who wants to do it all himself or to get all the credit for doing it."
—*Andrew Carnegie*

__ **Neglecting Self-Care:** I have often tried—and failed—to squeeze more hours out of each day. Invariably, I would be paying for it later on in the week. Remember to take care of yourself. **You can't pour from an empty cup.** Prioritize sleep, healthy food, relaxation, and fun activities to recharge fully.

__ **Idealism Leading to Disappointment:** Our ideals and high expectations sometimes set us up for disappointment when reality falls short. That's OK. Stay flexible; it allows for surprises to happen.

__ **Impracticality:** Living in a world of ideas and possibilities, we sometimes lose sight of what is happening around us. There's a time to stop dreaming, stop anticipating, and start creating. Stay practical and take action!

__ **Overcommitment:** We know we can skillfully execute any task that comes our way, which can lead us to bite off more than we can chew. Choose only worthy causes and practice saying 'No'! You cannot solve all the world's problems by yourself anyway. Learn to delegate. You may find people thrilled and waiting to be invited to join your endeavor!

__ **People Pleasing:** We're altruistic, often putting others' needs ahead of our own. It isn't entirely selfless, of course. Helping others rewards us with feeling great, which boosts our confidence. If we habitually aim to please people to avoid disagreements, we must realize that conflict isn't always bad. Sometimes, it's necessary for growth and progress. It's all about balancing, maintaining harmony, and standing up for what you believe in.

"Perfectionism is the silent assassin of creativity.
Dare to let go and watch innovation flourish."
—*Anonymous*

___ **Perfectionism:** Many of us turned into an ENFJ personality due to diminished self-confidence tracing back to our childhood. Perfectionism lasts only a split second before a situation is no longer perfect. So, trying to be perfect is the most significant waste of time, energy, and talent. **Aim for practicality instead.**

___ **Intense:** To some people, we will come off as a bit "intense." Even though we mean well, not everyone is ready or interested in making the necessary changes. Accept that. They'll find the right teacher when ready.

___ **Needing to Be Right**: Our well-intentioned desire to lead, control situations, and provide guidance can hinder not only our growth but also the growth of others. It is essential to confront our underlying insecurities since, coupled with negative thoughts, this tendency can outright harm us.

___ **Condescendence:** No matter how well we mean and how skilled we are, we should make sure not to let our offering of advice come off as condescending. Ask people the right questions. This allows *them* to discover the answers themselves. It will anchor the information and instill habits better than if you gave them the answers. Let them participate.

When we acknowledge and embrace these areas for improvement, we can start to turn some of these weaknesses into strengths. Imagine saying "No" becoming your superpower!

Progress takes time, so don't expect to be perfect overnight. In fact, don't expect to be perfect *at all!* Expect to be growing continually and enjoy the journey.

But you already know that, right?

Now, do it!

*"Integrity is choosing your thoughts and actions
based on values rather than personal gain."*
—*Chris Karcher*

Core Values

We have many moral values that we live by.

Rate from highest to lowest (5 to 1; leave blank if it doesn't apply) the **importance** of the values below. Circle the ranking if you've only just now become aware of it:

___ **Helpfulness:** We are naturally attuned to the emotions of others and often prioritize understanding and supporting them.

___ **Authenticity:** We value honesty, genuineness, and the ability to express feelings and thoughts openly.

___ **Loyalty:** We appreciate people who are loyal, keep their promises, and earn trust through their actions.

___ **Integrity:** We value adhering to a robust moral code and demonstrating honesty and consistency in our actions.

___ **Honesty:** We are resolved to be right, even if it implies admitting our mistakes or earlier misperceptions.

___ **Accountability:** We take responsibility for our actions and are accountable for our commitments.

___ **Spiritual Growth:** We are interested in mystery and seek to uncover life's hidden meaning and workings.

___ **Personal Growth:** We value any possible opportunity for self-improvement and seek to continuously learn and evolve as individuals.

___ **Positive Impact:** We have a deep-seated desire to positively impact the world around us.

"Values are like fingerprints. Nobody's are the same, but you leave them all over everything you do."
—*Elvis Presley*

___ **Altruism:** We find fulfillment in helping people overcome challenges and achieve their goals

___ **Positivity:** We encourage others to maintain a realistic but positive outlook, as we know that the negative never holds any solutions.

___ **Harmony:** We value cooperation and collaboration and often work to build consensus and resolve conflicts.

___ **Acceptance:** We embrace diversity and work to understand and respect the differences in others.

___ **Social Justice:** We value fairness, the well-being, and inclusivity of marginalized or disadvantaged individuals and groups

"*Good, better, best. Never let it rest.*
Until your good is better, and your better is best."
—*Saint Jerome*

Key Motivational Drivers

We have key motivational drivers that make all we do worthwhile and directly impact our happiness and fulfillment. Having these met will push us to do even better.

Rate from highest to lowest (5 to 1; leave blank if it doesn't apply) the **importance** of each driver below. Circle it if you have only just now become aware of it.

___ **Fame and Recognition:** Being in the spotlight, receiving praise and attention for efforts and accomplishments.

___ **Impact and Influence:** Seeing the immediate impact of our actions.

___ **Uniqueness and Being a Change Agent:** Being the one who is uniquely qualified to make a difference.

___ **Tasked with Responsibility:** Being chosen to fulfill an important responsibility and be responsible for the results.

___ **Mastery and Achievement:** Accomplishing our goals and advancing our skillset.

___ **Growth and Learning:** Continuous self-improvement.

___ **Creativity and Expression:** Expressing our ideas and emotions in unique ways.

___ **Altruism and Contribution:** Helping others and contributing to society.

___ **Cooperation and Harmony:** Fostering harmonious and collaborative relationships.

Each chapter will bring us closer to our ideal future.

"Be there for others, but never leave yourself behind."
—*Dodinksy*

Charting Your Ideal Future (Part 1)

- List your **highest-rated strengths** (5–4s or 4–3s). If you have too many, narrow it down to what is most important!

_____ _____

_____ _____

_____ _____

_____ _____

_____ _____

- Which strengths were you **previously unaware** of?

_____ _____

_____ _____

_____ _____

- How well are these being **utilized in your current work?**

_____

_____

_____

- List the **character weaknesses** (5–4s or 4–3s) that had a higher-than-expected impact on you.

_____ _____

_____ _____

"All your dreams are within reach,
no matter how big or crazy they might seem."
—*Jeannette Maw*

- How will you, from now on, **lower their impact** on you?

_____

_____

_____

_____

_____

_____

- List your **most important core values** (5–4s or 4–3s) when working for an organization or with others. If you have too many, narrow it down to what is most important!

_____   _____

_____   _____

_____   _____

_____   _____

_____   _____

- List your **most important motivational drivers** (5–4s or 4–3s). List them in order of importance.

_____   _____

_____   _____

_____   _____

_____   _____

_____   _____

*"Your work is to discover your world and then
with all your heart give yourself to it."*
—*Buddha*

- Which **insights and lessons** can you already draw from all of this that could guide your career decision?

_____

_____

_____

_____

_____

_____

_____

_____

_____

"Difficulties break some men but make others."
—*Nelson Mandela*

— Case Study: The Troubleshooter

Andre never felt like he fit in as a child. He struggled in school and had run-ins with the law. After many years of soul-searching, he discovered his ENFJ personality type in his late 20s.

Reading about his natural empathy, motivational abilities, and insightfulness resonated profoundly and gave him a new sense of purpose. He realized he could use these strengths to guide youth who were on similar troubled paths that he had been on.

Though he didn't have a background in counseling, he volunteered as a mentor for at-risk teens. The profound connections Andre formed, and his tangible impact on the kids' lives were incredibly rewarding. Soon, he returned to school to get certified as a youth counselor.

Though he had struggled for years to find his professional calling, once Andre tapped into his ENFJ talents, he discovered the fulfillment he had been seeking.

"It is impossible to live without failing at something unless you live so cautiously that you might as well not have lived at all, in which case you have failed by default."
—J.K. Rowling

Chapter 2 |
Motivations

According to Psychologist David Keirsey, only 2% to 5% of all people have our personality type, making it the second rarest personality in the world. I know. Sorry! But, yes, you *are* pretty special, and nowhere is it more evident than in your motivations.

Since they're primarily the result of our experiences in life, they are very different for each of us.

The questions on the pages ahead will provide you with more clarity, but reading the note below is crucial!

⚠ **Important**

Before you continue, **set aside at least 90 minutes** to answer the questions in this chapter.

You *do* want to find the path forward finally, right?

Great! Flip this page if you have time now. If not, then see you tomorrow!

BEST ENFJ EVER

"Trust yourself. You know more than you think you do."
—Benjamin Spock

You will notice that related questions have been rephrased in slightly different ways and listed in a specific order to help you gain additional insights.

For some, answers to the question about *purpose* come quickly. Others may find these more challenging and come back to them after completing the other questions. Whichever way you go about them, take your time, as they are some of the most vital questions in this book.

Don't overthink your answers. Write down the first thing that comes to mind.

It's a good idea to keep this book close by and look at your answers once every three months. People with ambitious goals often choose to review them monthly to stay on track.

As you change and grow, so will your answers. Retaking the questionnaire will provide insights about when it's a good time to pivot.

◎* **Progress Tracking**

Go ahead and set these reminders on your phone first:

Review ENFJ Motivation Answers
Recurring
Every month / Every three months / Every six months

Retake ENFJ Motivation Questionnaire
Recurring
Every year (preferably NOT the first two weeks of January)

Now that's out of the way, let's get you on track to where you *really* want to be!

"Your vision will become clear only when you can look into your own heart. Who looks outside, dreams; who looks inside, awakes."
—*Carl Jung*

Purpose

- What do you **want for yourself?**

_____

_____

_____

_____

_____

_____

_____

_____

- What do you **want for the people who are close to you?**

_____

_____

_____

_____

_____

_____

_____

_____

"You've got to think about big things
while you're doing small things,
so that all the small things
go in the right direction."
—Alvin Toffler

- How do you want to **make a difference** in the world?

  _____

  _____

  _____

  _____

  _____

  _____

- What kind of **legacy** do you want to leave behind?

  _____

  _____

  _____

  _____

  _____

- Which **big or small problems in the world** annoy you and need to be solved?

  _____

  _____

  _____

  _____

  _____

"*Never look down to test the ground before taking your next step. Only he who keeps his eye fixed on the far horizon will find the right road.*"
—*Dag Hammarskjöld*

- What are you **interested** in that could play a big or small part **in solving them?**

_____

_____

_____

_____

_____

_____

_____

_____

- Who do you **aspire** to be or be like, or who do you look up to, and why?

_____ _____

_____ _____

_____ _____

_____ _____

_____ _____

_____ _____

_____ _____

_____ _____

_____ _____

"*The price of anything is the amount of life you exchange for it.*"
—Henry David Thoreau

Work-Life Balance

- Do you prefer a **fast-paced** or **relaxed** work environment?

  _____

- Do you prefer a **structured** or **time-flexible** environment?

  _____

- Do you prefer **specializing** or **dabbling** in new things?

  _____

Interpersonal Dynamics

- Do you prefer to work in a **team** setting or **independently?**

  _____

  _____

  _____

- What does **your ideal work environment** look like?

  _____

  _____

  _____

  _____

  _____

*"Don't tell me where your priorities are.
Show me where you spend your money and
I'll tell you what they are."*
—*James W. Frick*

Autonomy & Ownership

- **NOT** considering financial rewards, do you prefer to be an **employee**, **manager**, **owner**, or **co-owner?** Why?

_____

_____

_____

_____

Financial Priorities

- How important are **salary** and **financial stability** to you?

_____

- Are you willing **to make financial sacrifices** to pursue your passion?

_____

- What do you **ideally WANT to earn?** Why?

_____

_____

_____

_____

_____

_____

"Time you enjoy wasting is not wasted time."
—Marthe Troly-Curtin

Skills & Talents

- **What are you good at?** What skills or talents make you feel good? What do people ask you for help with?

_____ _____

_____ _____

_____ _____

_____ _____

_____ _____

_____ _____

- **What have you always wanted to do or be good at**, but something got in the way? What has held you back so far?

_____ _____

_____ _____

_____ _____

_____ _____

_____ _____

- What do you **want to learn more about?**

_____ _____

_____ _____

_____ _____

_____ _____

"It's not always your skill level. It's always your passion and enthusiasm that makes you stand out from the crowd."

—*Anonymous*

Passions & Interests

- Which **causes** or **industries** excite you?

  _____   _____

  _____   _____

  _____   _____

- What are you **passionate** about? (Workwise)

  _____   _____

  _____   _____

  _____   _____

  _____   _____

- What are you **passionate** about? (Hobbies)

  _____   _____

  _____   _____

  _____   _____

  _____   _____

- What are you **passionate** about? (Other interests)

  _____   _____

  _____   _____

  _____   _____

  _____   _____

"Listen to your intuition.
It will tell you everything you need to know."
—Anthony J. D'Angelo

If you skipped the questions on *Purpose*, go back and complete those now. Ideally, go through the questions multiple times to gain more clarity.

⚞ Crossroads

When you encounter obstacles in life, you may be at a crossroads. Revisit this chapter to gain additional insights. You may discover that your motivations and passions have shifted, necessitating you to make a career change to stay fulfilled.

You're on a path of eternal growth, after all!

"Follow your passion. The rest will attend to itself.
If I can do it, anybody can do it. It's possible.
And it's your turn. So, go for it.
It's never too late to become what you always
wanted to be in the first place."
—J. Michael Straczynski

Charting Your Ideal Future (Part 2)

- Make a **quick, one-page summary** of what you've written in this chapter so far. What have you discovered?

_____

_____

_____

_____

_____

_____

_____

_____

_____

_____

_____

_____

_____

_____

_____

_____

_____

"Whatever you're thinking, think bigger!"
—*Tony Hsieh*

- Take 10–15 minutes to **describe your ideal career and life** if anything were possible. Dream big! Be as specific as possible—describe a typical day or week in this perfect career, from the moment you wake up until the time you go to bed. Also, write down **why it matters to you.**

_____

_____

_____

_____

_____

_____

_____

_____

_____

_____

_____

_____

_____

_____

_____

_____

"The only way to discover the limits of the possible is to go beyond them into the impossible."
—*Arthur C. Clarke*

"You get what you focus on, so focus on what you want."
—*Steve Mehr*

"Your next chapter is going to be amazing!"
—*Anonymous*

- Lastly, taking into account your current financial situation and obligations, write down some **potential opportunities** or **midway careers you currently have in mind** that could provide income while also moving you closer to your ideal. These could be full-time jobs, freelance work, online side businesses, etc.

_____

_____

_____

_____

"Be strong. Don't be a follower, always do your own thing and follow your heart."
—Jennifer Lawrence

Chapter 3 |
Fulfilling Careers

Our versatility allows us, like no other, to craft careers that fit well with our interests and life purpose.

It can be as staff or in a management position in an organization. Some of us very visibly take the reins as CEO. Others remain in the background as the owners of a growing business empire. Still, others are happiest self-employed and as the go-to person in their close-knit community. And some brave ones abandon their old life for good and find the most meaning in volunteering in faraway places.

We can be actors, dancers, fashion designers, writers, coaches, experts, managers, media personalities, influencers, kingmakers, or spiritual leaders who build faithful communities of followers.

With such a wide range of skills and talents, there has to be overlap. That's not a problem at all. We often skillfully carve out a combination of a few different careers for ourselves and find it easy to apply knowledge gained in one industry to a different one!

Don't fall into the trap of becoming a 'jack of all trades, master of none' though! For many ENFJs, nurturing our passion and

"You must learn to trust that there is a future waiting for you that is beyond what you might be able to grasp at this present moment."
—*Anonymous*

honing our skills will demand time and practice. But structure, direction, and good habits are required too to turn those lofty dreams into reality.

Over the years, and as a result of my and other ENFJs' experiences, I've devised a system that rates how well certain professions fit with our personality type on a scale of 100. It will help you make better career decisions.

Any value of 80 or higher indicates that it is a good to excellent match. Careers in the 70s are less compatible as they lack one or more aspects important to ENFJs. A job may be highly analytical or solitary and score just 70. Yet, when combined with another role, e.g., one that allows plenty of personal interaction, our social needs may still be met.

Now is the moment where you can apply the clarity you have gained from *Chapter One* and *Chapter Two* to identify your career sweet spot—the place where your natural talents, passions, and the world's needs intersect.

After the profile of Sarah, you will find an extensive list of compatible careers grouped around our ENFJ values and strengths. It is NOT meant to be the end-all list of compatible jobs, but it is carefully crafted to show you all that's available once you get clear and decide to go after what you deserve. It also aims to inspire you to mix and match and dream up entirely new careers with the characteristics of your choosing.

Recognizing that you may be unaware of many potential career options that fit your strengths and interests, maintain an open mind as you review the list of recommended careers.

"*Your time is limited, so don't waste it living someone else's life. Don't be trapped by dogma—which is living with the results of other people's thinking.*"
—*Steve Jobs*

With a **pencil**, put a checkmark before careers that spark your interest or curiosity, not just what you *can do* or what you're good at. We'll narrow the list down in *Chapter Five*, but **try not to go overboard—top picks only** of what you'd really enjoy and perhaps a few midway jobs that align with your interests.

If your brain is wired like mine, and you have plenty of diverse interests, start by diagonally crossing out checkboxes of uninteresting careers. Do so GENTLY, as they should not become distractions to your interests. This process of elimination helps us achieve a sense of peace, focus, and of making progress, and that's precisely what we need!

Don't overanalyze at this stage—instead, go with your gut! **Go after what you want** and know full well that **you will have to put the work in to get there.** That's life.

Have confidence.

When ENFJs find their power, anything is possible!

"If you could only sense how important you are to the lives of those you meet, how important you can be to the people you may never even dream of.
There is something of yourself that you leave at every meeting with another person."
—Fred Rogers

— ENFJ Profile: Sarah

Sarah, a mental health counselor, shares what's rewarding about her career.

"I became a counselor to help people overcome life's challenges and traumas.

My clients can bare their souls and feel heard during our sessions. They know they enter a safe space where there is no judgment. I've gone through a lot in life myself. It isn't always easy.

I'm not looking to give them a quick, short-lived fix. Instead, I allow them to be themselves, and we brainstorm solutions together. They feel that they're actively participating in the solution process. At the same time, it gives me more information about how they think, what they like, and potential fears that aren't immediately visible on the surface.

That's how I craft personalized treatment plans for each person's unique situation. I'm creating a doorway that's giving them a chance to leave the past behind and courageously choose a better path."

Sarah uses her empathy, insight, communication skills, and creativity to empower others on their healing journeys. She's been there herself, so they're in capable hands.

And so are you! Are you ready to discover all the possible careers waiting for you?

Follow me!

"To love and be loved is to feel the sun from both sides."
—David Viscott

1: Helping & Service Careers

Our skills and personalities gracefully align with careers centered around helping, understanding, and inspiring others. Drawing energy and joy from teaching, counseling, and healthcare, we find fulfillment in supporting personal growth and well-being—the very core of our motivations.

Guidance Counselor, Teacher, and Nurse exemplify some of these paths with compatibility scores of 100 and 95. However, our broad scope of interests may lead us to consider other options. Language Teacher—even though it has a slightly lower score of 80—can be just as appealing to an ENFJ with a passion for languages, cultural exchange, and traveling.

Our ENFJ essence echoes in counseling, community leadership, and humanitarian work. Our communication talents, leadership, idealism, and selfless nature make us powerful advocates, presenting us with a vast array of opportunities where we can make a meaningful difference.

Get your pencil ready.

It's time to take your life into your own hands.

"We rise by lifting others."
—*Robert Ingersoll*

EDUCATION

Careers in education appeal to our passion for nurturing growth and development. As teachers, counselors, librarians, and school administrators, we can pass on knowledge and inspire students to reach their full potential.

- [ ] Guidance Counselor **100**
- [ ] Primary-Secondary Teacher **95**
- [ ] Language Teacher 80
- [ ] Adult Literacy Teacher 85
- [ ] Special Education Teacher **95**
- [ ] College Lecturer 85
- [ ] University Professor 75
- [ ] Librarian 80
- [ ] School Psychologist **90**
- [ ] Principal **95**
- [ ] Faculty Dean 80

"The simple act of caring is heroic."
—*Edward Albert*

HEALTHCARE

Healthcare careers allow us to care for people directly and positively impact their well-being. As nurses, therapists, counselors, and more, we can provide hands-on support guided by compassion. We are excellent caregivers and know that our presence is as much a healing factor as any medicine or medical instrument.

- [ ] Health Educator **90**
- [ ] Dietitian **90**
- [ ] Nutritionist **90**
- [ ] Dental Hygienist 75
- [ ] Speech Pathologist **90**
- [ ] Audiologist 85
- [ ] Nurse/Nurse Practitioner **95**
- [ ] EMT and Paramedic 70
- [ ] Physical Therapist **95**
- [ ] Chiropractor **90**
- [ ] Fitness Trainer 80
- [ ] Geriatric Care Manager **90**

"Be a lamp, or a lifeboat, or a ladder.
Help someone's soul heal."
—*Rumi*

COUNSELING AND THERAPY

Here, we can leverage our exceptional listening and people skills and vast and in-depth specialized knowledge. As therapists, counselors, and social workers, we are ideally suited to help individuals navigate life-altering personal challenges.

- ☐ Career Counselor **100**
- ☐ Crisis Counselor **95**
- ☐ Trauma Counselor **95**
- ☐ Emotional Wellness Counselor **100**
- ☐ Mental Health Counselor **100**
- ☐ Substance Abuse Counselor **95**
- ☐ Peer Support Counselor **100**
- ☐ Rehabilitation Counselor **95**
- ☐ Hospice Counselor **95**
- ☐ Marriage and Family Therapist **95**
- ☐ Child Care Worker **95**
- ☐ Social Worker **100**
- ☐ Occupational Therapist **95**
- ☐ Art Therapist 85

"*Caring about your career is not
working the most hours.
It's caring the most in the hours you work.*"
—Anthony Melchiorri

FOOD AND HOSPITALITY

We excel in food and hospitality roles by creating welcoming environments and ensuring patrons have the most memorable experience. Our charm, attention to detail, and ability to anticipate others' needs make us well-suited for roles such as tour guides, restaurant managers, and hotel owners.

- [ ] Barista 70
- [ ] Waiter/Waitress 70
- [ ] Caterer 75
- [ ] Restaurant Manager 75
- [ ] Property Manager 85
- [ ] Front-of-House 80
- [ ] Cruise Director **90**
- [ ] Travel Agent 80
- [ ] Tour Guide **90**
- [ ] Flight Attendant 85

"Too often we underestimate the power of a touch, a smile, a kind word, a listening ear, an honest compliment, or the smallest act of caring, all of which have the potential to turn a life around."
—*Leo Buscaglia*

SPIRITUAL WORK

Spiritual work appeals to our sense of meaning and values. As clergy, religious workers, and youth pastors, we fulfill our altruistic motivations to help others find purpose and connection as well.

- [ ] Religious Worker 85
- [ ] Clergy Member 80
- [ ] Spiritual Leader 80
- [ ] Pastoral Counselor **95**
- [ ] Youth Pastor **95**

NON-PROFIT WORK

Working in the non-profit sector lets us champion the causes we believe in. Our ability to inspire and mobilize people is a tremendous asset in raising awareness and funds! These unique skills can secure long-term, well-paying jobs.

When we find an organization that aligns well with our values, we quickly reach ever higher levels of success, benefiting not just ourselves but everyone involved.

- [ ] Director 85
- [ ] Program Manager 85
- [ ] Advocacy Specialist **95**
- [ ] Fundraiser Coordinator **100**
- [ ] Crisis Hotline Counselor **95**
- [ ] Humanitarian Aid Worker **90**
- [ ] Refugee Resettlement Coordinator **95**

"*We make a living by what we get, but we make a life by what we give.*"
—*Winston Churchill*

COMMUNITY ENGAGEMENT

Community engagement is where we shine most. We possess a unique ability to see deeper than surface level, negotiate win-wins, bring people of different stripes together, and foster a tight sense of community. Union representatives, organizers, and diplomats all play vital roles in improving their community and supporting its members.

- [ ] Activist 70
- [ ] Union Representative 75
- [ ] Liaison **90**
- [ ] Diplomat 85
- [ ] Diplomatic Relations Officer **90**
- [ ] Community Leader **95**
- [ ] Community Organizer **90**
- [ ] Community Outreach Coordinator **95**

"Unless someone like you cares a whole awful lot, nothing is going to get better. It's not."
—Dr. Seuss

POLITICS AND GOVERNMENT

In politics and government, we affect change on a large scale. Our leadership abilities and integrity can lead to successful careers as political campaign managers or public policy consultants. If we go on and decide to burst into the—often dark—realm of politics, we have to make sure we do so for the right reasons: to affect meaningful change and not out of a need for purely financial gains or the spotlight. Before starting such an endeavor, it will be good to surround ourselves with a solid team of people with similar values and high integrity.

- [ ] Policy Advisor 80
- [ ] Campaign Manager **90**
- [ ] Community Relations Director **100**
- [ ] Politician 80

LAW AND MEDIATION

Legal work centered on mediation and championing justice or civil rights resonates with our values. As attorneys and defenders of the greater good, we help resolve conflicts and counsel others constructively. The higher impact our mediation can bring, the more it appeals to us.

- [ ] Lawyer 75
- [ ] Family Law Attorney 85
- [ ] Civil Rights Lawyer **90**
- [ ] Public Defender 85
- [ ] Mediator **95**

"Think lightly of yourself and deeply of the world."
—*Miyamoto Musashi*

CIVIL SERVICES

We have a knack for seeing the big picture as well as the minute details. Combined with our quick, decisive nature and desire to help in moments of crisis, we are bound to become lifesavers in one way or another.

☐ Crisis Intervention Specialist **90**

☐ Emergency Relief Worker **90**

☐ Emergency Response Coordinator 80

☐ Hostage Negotiator 75

"*The interesting thing about coaching is that you have to trouble the comfortable and comfort the troubled.*"
—*Ric Charlesworth*

2: Coaching & Mentorship

Careers in this field are a natural fit for ENFJs, often described as natural teachers and mentors.

As coaches and consultants who improve one's business, life, relationships, and more, we empower others to set, achieve, and surpass new goals. Our encouragement and wisdom help clients overcome challenges, develop new skills, and navigate life's most challenging terrains. Even without an official title, we will often mentor and coach people throughout our lives in some capacity.

Unsurprisingly, Relationship Coach—with a compatibility score of 100—stands out, as relationships are central to all we do. Even a lower-scoring role such as Business Coach can be fulfilling if we have experience in business operations and find a great company with warm people to work with.

Coaching and mentorship offer many fulfilling career paths for those wishing to help others grow while staying lifelong students ourselves.

- [ ] Leadership Training Facilitator **90**
- [ ] Team Building Coach **95**
- [ ] Public Speaking Coach **90**
- [ ] Business Coach 80
- [ ] Executive Coach **90**
- [ ] Leadership Coach **90**
- [ ] Career Coach **95**
- [ ] Life Coach **95**
- [ ] Relationship Coach **100**

"Strong cultures start with great leaders who build organizations that reflect their values."
—*Simon Sinek*

3: Leadership & Management

Often blessed with charisma and focus, we thrive in leadership and management positions. For us, effective leadership isn't about power—it's about empowering, mentoring even.

As executives, managers, and directors, we are good at identifying the strengths and weaknesses of our team members. Our inspirational leadership style and ability to intuitively delegate the right tasks ensure everyone is working to their highest potential.

- [ ] Project Manager 80
- [ ] Program Manager 75
- [ ] Department Manager 75
- [ ] Operations Manager 75
- [ ] Team Manager 80
- [ ] Operations Director/COO **90**
- [ ] Executive Director/CEO 85
- [ ] Advisory Board Member 80
- [ ] Ethics Officer 80

*"The only thing worse than training your employees
and having them leave is not training them
and having them stay."*
—Henry Ford

4: Business Operations

When we find a business that aligns with our values and motivations, a business operations career allows us to employ a wide array of our unique talents.

These positions necessitate strong organizational skills, attention to detail, multi-tasking abilities, strategic thinking, creative problem-solving, and team coordination—all areas where ENFJs naturally excel.

One of the top matches in this category is the HR Manager role, with a compatibility score of 95. Here, we can leverage our deep understanding of human dynamics to ensure the workplace is supportive and fair.

As long as we feel appreciated and see opportunities for growth, a career in business operations can be highly rewarding, allowing us to contribute substantially to our organization's success.

"Quality is never an accident; it is always the result of high intention, sincere effort, intelligent direction, and skillful execution."
—William A. Foster

OPERATIONS

Our keen eye for every small detail and ability to coordinate various tasks make us invaluable in roles that require managing resources, overseeing logistics, and solving complex problems. We take pride in ensuring that everything runs smoothly and efficiently.

- ☐ Receptionist **90**
- ☐ Executive Assistant **95**
- ☐ Office Manager 75
- ☐ Event Coordinator **95**
- ☐ Team Facilitator **90**
- ☐ HR Manager **95**
- ☐ HR Specialist **90**
- ☐ Recruiter 85
- ☐ Corporate Trainer 85
- ☐ Knowledge Management Specialist 75
- ☐ Learning and Development Specialist **95**
- ☐ Psychologist **90**

*"In the end, all business operations can be reduced
to three words: people, product, and profits.
People come first.
Unless you've got a good team,
you can't do much with the other two."*
—*Lee Iacocca*

SALES AND MARKETING

Some love sales and marketing, while others hate it, primarily due to earlier real or perceived experiences with salespeople.

People considering this career should ask themselves what they hope to get from the "deal"? Is it fame? Is it money? Or, is it the immense satisfaction of helping people find the product or service they need and building strong relationships with clients?

ENFJs in this industry experiencing less success can increase their luck by focusing less on the money and more on providing the absolute best service. The total sum of better service and a better experience often leads to higher company profits, resulting in higher income and prestige.

☐ Online Marketer 75

☐ Brand Strategist 75

☐ Advertising Executive 75

☐ Consultant 85

☐ Business Development Manager 85

☐ Customer Success Manager **95**

☐ Customer Service Manager **90**

☐ Marketing Manager 80

☐ Sales Manager 80

☐ Sales Representative 85

☐ Strategic Planner 75

"There are no traffic jams along the extra mile."
—*Zig Ziglar*

CUSTOMER EXPERIENCE

With a knack for understanding people's needs and exceeding their expectations, ENFJs will ensure that every customer interaction is positive and memorable!

- [ ] Helpdesk Support Specialist 80
- [ ] Customer Support Representative **90**
- [ ] Ombudsman 80

RESEARCH AND ANALYSIS

While research and analysis roles are generally less appealing to ENFJs, they can still be a good match if the organization fits well with our values and contributes to a bigger goal. We enjoy diving deep into data to uncover insights and understand how all the different pieces fit the puzzle.

A genuine interest in what the organization brings to the world is crucial, not just because one is skilled or "for the money only," as we hate rote, meaningless tasks.

- [ ] Data Scientist 85
- [ ] Blockchain Architect 80
- [ ] Competitive Analyst 85
- [ ] Market Analyst 80
- [ ] Trends Analyst 85
- [ ] Policy Analyst 80
- [ ] Program Evaluator 80
- [ ] Social Impact Analyst **90**
- [ ] Business Strategist 80

"If you want to build a ship, don't drum up the men to gather wood, divide the work and give orders. Instead, teach them to yearn for the vast and endless sea."
—*Antoine de Saint-Exupéry*

5: Communications

Careers in communication enable us to harness our more advanced verbal skills, engaging audiences effectively. Roles such as Public Relations specialists, journalists, writers, and spokespeople allow us to disseminate ideas, weave compelling narratives, and advocate causes we deeply resonate with.

The position of Communications Director, boasting a compatibility score of 95, emerges as an outstanding choice. It enables us to craft and uphold a favorable public persona for the organizations we choose to represent.

The role of Technical Writer, with a lower score of 70, could be suitable for those who excel at simplifying intricate information. Combining this solitary role with another position that offers significant human interaction is highly recommended, though.

"To effectively communicate, we must realize that we are all different in the way we perceive the world and use this understanding as a guide to our communication with others."
—*Tony Robbins*

PUBLIC RELATIONS

Their often passionate storytelling and ability to connect with diverse audiences make ENFJs well-suited for public relations specialist or communications manager roles.

☐ PR Executive **90**   ☐ Motivational Speaker **95**

☐ PR Manager **90**   ☐ Interpreter 85

☐ PR Account Manager 75   ☐ Translator 75

☐ Speechwriter 80

☐ Corporate Spokesperson 85

☐ Media Relations Specialist 75

☐ Communications Director **95**

☐ Community Rel. Manager **95**

JOURNALISM

Plenty of ENFJs love the spotlight. We are also intrigued by mystery. Our curiosity, uncanny ability to connect the dots, and excellent communication skills make us successful journalists and reporters. We use our platform to uncover significant news events, educate the public, and advocate for truth and transparency. Some of us will go on to host our own shows in a more independent capacity later on.

☐ Investigative Journalist 70   ☐ Journalist 85

☐ Foreign Correspondent 75   ☐ Reporter 85

☐ Photojournalist 75   ☐ News Anchor 85

☐ Multimedia Journalist 75

"*We write to taste life twice,
in the moment and in retrospect.*"
—*Anaïs Nin*

WRITER

We crave expressing ourselves, so a writing career can prove fulfilling. Whether by crafting mesmerizing stories, insightful articles, or any other type of engaging content, we use our writing to connect with readers, share our perspectives, and make waves.

Writing, though more solitary, allows for plenty of creativity. Writers should combine it with less isolated tasks to stay tethered to the outside world. It will enable us to recharge our batteries and draw real-life inspiration.

- [ ] Technical Writer 70
- [ ] Content Writer 70
- [ ] Columnist 75
- [ ] Copywriter 85
- [ ] Screenplay Writer 75
- [ ] Script Writer 85
- [ ] Feature Writer 80
- [ ] Copy Editor 75
- [ ] Editor 85
- [ ] Author 85
- [ ] Novelist 85

"Every great dream begins with a dreamer.
Always remember, you have within you the strength,
the patience, and the passion to reach for the stars
to change the world."
—*Harriet Tubman*

6: Creative, Media, & Artistic Careers

The expansive world of creative, media, and artistic careers is a playground for ENFJs' many exceptional abilities.

In the limelight or behind the scenes, roles like actor, fashion designer, content creator, radio host, and creative director underline the versatility of ENFJs. We might be setting the stage alight or stirring up a digital revolution while fostering connections and understanding with people at a deeper level.

Amidst the diversity of these careers, we find ourselves at the heart of the creative process, shaping experiences, forging bonds, and resonating with audiences worldwide. Our skill set, flexibility, empathetic nature, and visionary mindset make this field fertile ground for meaningful and satisfying work.

"You don't take a photograph. You make it."
—*Ansel Adams*

PERFORMING ARTS

Our ability to understand and evoke emotions can turn us into successful actors, dancers, musicians, photographers, or comedians. We prosper even more when live on stage, where we can connect directly with the audience.

☐ Actor **90**

☐ Comedian 85

☐ Singer 85

☐ Musician 80

☐ Dancer 85

☐ Choreographer **90**

☐ Acrobat 80

☐ Magician 80

☐ Mentalist **90**

VISUAL ARTS AND DESIGN

Here, we aim to stimulate emotions and enhance people's lives and experiences. Visual Arts and Design lets us turn our creativity, perspective, and problem-solving skills into impactful designs, functional products, user-friendly interfaces, or efficient spaces that people will love!

☐ Photographer 85

☐ Curator 80

☐ Graphic Designer 75

☐ Interior Designer 75

☐ Fashion Designer 85

☐ Web Designer 70

"Content is fire, social media is gasoline."
—*Jay Baer*

CONTENT CREATION

Content creation provides us with additional platforms to share our ideas, experiences, and insights with the world.

☐ Blogger 70

☐ Vlogger 70

☐ Social Media Manager 80

☐ Performer 85

☐ Content Creator 85

🎙 Get Started Today

Check out the related *Online Services* section later for even more careers that can be started as a side gig!

MEDIA PRODUCTION

Understanding what resonates with people is valuable in roles that involve producing engaging TV shows, films, or digital content that reaches a broad audience.

☐ Media Production/Assistant 75

☐ Show Host (Podcast, YouTube, etc.) 85

☐ Radio and TV Host **90**

"To be authentic, you have to have the courage to be imperfect."

—*Brené Brown*

INFLUENCER AND BRANDING

As online personalities, ENFJs leverage their understanding of people and trends to build strong brands and loyal followings.

- ☐ TikToker 70
- ☐ Podcaster 85
- ☐ YouTuber 85
- ☐ Brand Ambassador 75
- ☐ Influencer 70

CREATIVE DIRECTION

In Creative Direction, we can use our leadership skills and creative vision to guide and inspire our team. We oversee the entire creative process, ensure the results align with that vision, and craft compelling narratives that resonate with audiences worldwide.

- ☐ Film Director 80
- ☐ Theater Director 85
- ☐ Art Director **90**
- ☐ Creative Director **90**
- ☐ Creative Producer **95**

*"Do not wait: the time will never be 'just right.'
Start where you stand, and work with whatever tools
you may have at your command, and better tools
will be found as you go along."*
—*Napoleon Hill*

7: Self-Employment & Entrepreneurship

In self-employment and entrepreneurship, those of us who desire to carve our path and who have a strong vision and the drive to guide our business toward success can find lots of inspiration and satisfaction.

These careers provide them with the autonomy they often seek: to set their own rules, make all decisions aligned with their values, and see the immediate impact of their work.

The *Online Services* section is an exciting highlight later on in this category, where you can leverage your already vast knowledge and talents to build an online business that reaches a broad audience and can be operated from anywhere in the world. It's an excellent way to expand your impact and enjoy an online career's flexibility.

ENTREPRENEURSHIP

Entrepreneurship offers us the freedom and flexibility to create businesses that perfectly align with our core values. Our vision, leadership, and drive help us transform our ideas into exceptional, trend-setting products or services.

- [ ] Small Business Owner 75
- [ ] Startup Founder 80
- [ ] Entrepreneur 80
- [ ] Social Entrepreneur 85

"If you're not taking care of your customer, your competitor will."
—Bob Hooey

PERSONAL SERVICES

Experts in finding out what a client wants, we create personalized experiences that bring joy and convenience to our clients. These services don't require us to own any property to get started, so we often share a location with others at first.

- ☐ Makeup Artist 85
- ☐ Esthetician 70
- ☐ Cosmetologist 75
- ☐ Hairstylist 75
- ☐ Massage Therapist 80
- ☐ Spa Manager 85
- ☐ Pet Groomer 80
- ☐ Pet Walker 85
- ☐ Doula **90**
- ☐ Personal Trainer **90**
- ☐ Personal Stylist 85
- ☐ Personal Assistant **95**
- ☐ Wellness Counselor **90**
- ☐ Intuitive Counselor **90**
- ☐ Astrologer 80
- ☐ Psychic/Medium 75
- ☐ Shamanic Practitioner 80

- ☐ Hypnotist 80
- ☐ NLP Practitioner 85
- ☐ Energy Healer 85
- ☐ Meditation Teacher 85
- ☐ Mindfulness Teacher 85
- ☐ Yoga Teacher **90**
- ☐ Dance Instructor 85
- ☐ Herbalist 80
- ☐ Aromatherapist 85
- ☐ Health Coach 85
- ☐ Etiquette Consultant 85
- ☐ Feng Shui Consultant 85
- ☐ Landscaper 75
- ☐ Gardener 85

"*To be successful, you have to have your heart in your business, and your business in your heart.*
—*Sr. Thomas Watson*

LOCATION-BASED SERVICES

Those of us fully aligned with our passion and skills and willing to invest in renting or acquiring property can make it big in this setting. We thrive on owning the process, from ideation to execution, shaping businesses that resonate with our vision. Resolute in our commitment and with a fixed location, we are building a landmark rather than just a business.

- [ ] Baker 85
- [ ] Chocolatier 85
- [ ] Coffee Shop Owner 85
- [ ] Food Truck Owner 80
- [ ] Farmer's Market Manager **90**
- [ ] Eco-Tour Entrepreneur 85
- [ ] Travel Agency Owner 85
- [ ] Bed and Breakfast Owner 80
- [ ] Art Gallery Owner 85
- [ ] Boutique Owner 80
- [ ] Beauty Clinic Owner 80
- [ ] Fitness Studio Owner 85
- [ ] Wellness Studio Owner 85
- [ ] Resort Owner 75
- [ ] Event Planning Business Owner **90**
- [ ] Wedding Studio Owner **90**
- [ ] Jewelry Designer 85
- [ ] Concierge Service 80
- [ ] Conference Organizer 85
- [ ] Real Estate Agent **90**

*"Write down every single idea you have,
no matter how big or small."*
—*Richard Branson*

8: Online Services

We possess the skills, hobbies, and interests that allow us to start business ventures on the side of our regular employment career.

We can consolidate many of our talents and jobs listed earlier into a business that is our own and that we can manage from any location on the planet.

It can be in a teaching and mentoring capacity by creating and bringing innovative products and services to market, providing assistance and support, or being knowledge specialists in our own right.

BEST ENFJ EVER

"Your brand is the single most important investment you can make in your business."
—*Steve Forbes*

130

TEACHING AND MENTORING

Some of the most rewarding and lucrative careers are online coaching and consulting. For ENFJs, this is also one of the easiest industries to get into, as we are adept at turning abstract knowledge into practical steps that help our clients improve their skills, scale their businesses, or crank their personal lives up a notch.

☐ Online Coach **90**   ☐ Online Tutor **90**

☐ Online Mentor **90**   ☐ Online Counselor **90**

☐ Online Teacher **90**   ☐ Online Educator 85

PRODUCTS AND SERVICES

We establish our authority by curating news around our interests, publishing blogs or books, and converting our audience into coaching clients. Some of us find the most joy in the creative process, producing or curating unique designs or products to sell online. And then, some identify what the world needs and create innovative solutions, platforms, or services that generate monthly subscription fees. ENFJs are positioned like no other to enjoy the flexibility of an online business.

☐ Online Event Planner 85   ☐ Online Publisher **90**

☐ Online Webinar Producer 80   ☐ Online Curator **90**

☐ Online Course Creator 85   ☐ Online Site Owner 80

☐ Digital Product Creator 85   ☐ Online Store Owner 80

☐ Digital Service Creator 85

"The future of marketing is storytelling."
—*Seth Godin*

ONLINE MARKETING

While there are many better careers for ENFJs, I have decided to list these here because they can be a good choice if done right. The key is finding the best product in the market—the only one we are ready to associate our reputation with—and presenting it as the solution to our audience's challenges.

As integrity is paramount to ENFJs, affiliate marketing is often only used to supplement other online ventures such as blogging, coaching, or monthly subscription services, not as a career by itself.

☐ Affiliate Marketer 75

☐ Affiliate Manager 80

VIRTUAL ASSISTANCE

Our organizational skills, attention to detail, communication prowess, and ability to anticipate others' needs make us excellent virtual assistants and online community managers.

It is also an ideal job where we can grow our skillset, build a network, and feel great about the difference we make daily in people's lives.

☐ Virtual Assistant 85

☐ Online Community Manager **95**

☐ Online Customer Support Representative 85

"You are your greatest asset.
Put your time, effort, and money into training,
grooming, and encouraging your greatest asset."
—*Tom Hopkins*

SPECIALISTS AND RESEARCH

We are passionate about growth, learning, and discovering why things are how they are. Online specialist and research jobs allow us to use our accumulated expertise and conduct research relevant to our field from the comfort of our homes.

- [ ] Online Marketing Specialist 80
- [ ] Online Fundraising Specialist **95**
- [ ] Online Learning Specialist **90**
- [ ] Online Research Specialist 80
- [ ] Online Technology Specialist 85
- [ ] Online User Experience Specialist 85
- [ ] Social Media Strategist **90**
- [ ] Website Accessibility Specialist **90**
- [ ] Web Analytics Specialist 75

"Do less, with more focus."
—*Anonymous*

Charting Your Ideal Future (Part 3)

- **How many** careers did you check off in the complete list?

_____

- **If you checked off many,** ask yourself why.

_____

_____

- Would you **really** want to do all of them?

_____

- **Which careers, categories, and industries do you want to remove?** Use the eraser and afterward write *"I'm becoming more focused on what I really want."* on the line below.

_____

- **Which categories**, where you have only 1 or 2 careers checked, **are more difficult to let go of?** Why?

_____

_____

_____

_____

_____

_____

"Never give up on a dream just because of the time it will take to accomplish it. The time will pass anyway."
—Earl Nightingale

- **Which 5 careers** stood out to you as **solid matches?** Why?

_____

_____

_____

_____

_____

_____

_____

_____

_____

- Which **categories/industries** seem most appealing to you based on the number of jobs you've checked off?

_____

_____

_____

_____

_____

_____

_____

_____

Great job! That's it for this chapter!

"Your own self-realization is the greatest service you can render the world."
—*Ramana Maharshi*

— Case Study: Crafting Confidence

After college, Rebecca quickly moved up the corporate ladder in sales thanks to her charisma and people skills. However, the work felt soulless—she wanted to do something more meaningful. Rebecca used her keen fashion sense on weekends to advise friends on their styles. Their confidence skyrocketed after her makeovers— she had a gift!

She decided to take a risk and start an image consulting business, drawing on her ENFJ abilities to read people and situations. The autonomy of working for herself allowed Rebecca to build a company that was an authentic expression of her values, creativity, and talents.

Giving up the security of a stable corporate salary was frightening, but after seeing her first few clients transform, she was convinced it was the right thing to do. Years later, she runs a thriving consultancy helping executives present the most polished, commanding version of themselves.

She loves the freedom of being her own boss and the fulfillment that comes from using her talents to empower people to put their best selves forward.

"You've got to get up every morning with determination if you're going to go to bed with satisfaction."
—George Horace Lorimer

Chapter 4 |
Career Pitfalls

Often, we are self-sabotaging the great opportunities put right before us. Other times, we get stuck in a less-than-optimal job, especially when we're good at it! Watch your step.

The Career Selection Dilemma

While corporate paths can reward staff with a substantial paycheck and the prestige and recognition they crave, we often yearn for more. We must find organizations that align with our motivations and values for it to be all worthwhile.

Reviewing your list of values and motivations will clarify what to look for in an employer, career, or industry.

Too Much Choice

With the broad range of skills and talents, ENFJs do not suffer from a lack of choice but rather from *too much* of it. They must ensure that their quest for "the perfect career" doesn't lead to decision paralysis—**and starvation!**

"Beware of monotony; it's the mother of all deadliness."
—*Edith Wharton*

Not making any decision out of fear of missing out is worse! There is no one perfect career. In fact, there are many, and you'll likely move between them over time. Just look for one that aligns, get going, and don't be afraid to level up if a great new opportunity comes along!

"What if I'm just not feeling it in my current career?"

Soulless Monotony

ENFJs struggle in careers with monotonous and uninteresting work. It hinders their growth. We won't want to waste our time on the boring stuff. If there's no significant upside, move on!

Lack of Social Interaction

Even though we often need time to be alone with our thoughts, we need human interaction and to feel that our presence on this planet is meaningful. Social isolation not only kills our creativity. It kills our spirit as well!

Where Are Your Ethical Standards?!

For ENFJs, employment is more than a mere professional engagement; it's a personal connection that necessitates utmost integrity.

We grapple with business sectors that lack social responsibilities and that potentially cause harm to others. We will want to ensure that our organization's values align well with our own.

If you sometimes struggle to get out of bed, take stock of what it is that's making you feel unfulfilled.

BEST ENFJ EVER

*"People may spend their whole lives
climbing the ladder of success only to find,
once they reach the top, that the ladder
is leaning against the wrong wall."*
—*Thomas Merton*

Suboptimal Career Paths

Careers like the ones on the next page typically aren't a good match for ENFJs due to the nature of the work and the environment in which they are conducted.

As socially oriented, empathetic, and inspiring individuals, we thrive in roles where we can interact with and help others. We excel when we have opportunities to motivate, counsel, and lead people. At the same time, our work allows for creativity, self-expression, and alignment with our strong values. Autonomy and a dynamic, varied work environment are crucial for job satisfaction.

Careers like Military Officers, Law Enforcement, Factory Supervisors, and Power Plant Operators will require strict adherence to protocols, which might not provide the empathetic approach we prefer.

Jobs such as Accountants and IT Specialists require detail-oriented work—which ENFJs typically excel at—but are mostly solitary and systematic and do not resonate with our need for interpersonal interaction.

While creative and problem-solving, professions in engineering often lack this human-centered focus, too. Yet, they may still be a good fit with the proper organization that allows us to bring about innovative solutions the world needs.

Network Marketing is hardly *ever* a good choice, nor is any industry that ENFJs consider to lack integrity. The industry attempts to make "success replicable" by seeing every downline as a square peg and subsequently trying to fit them into a round hole. It is filled with people who have yet to learn what it takes to make the diverse personality types on their team succeed.

"Never be a prisoner of your past.
It was just a lesson, not a life sentence!"
—*Anonymous*

In the early days of starting my coaching career, I was approached to do Network Marketing. I liked some of the products, as well as the people aspect. But, as replication demands, you can't just love a few products; you need to profess your love for the whole range, even those you have no affinity with. Luckily, my business partner loved those products, which solved it for us, and our network was slowly growing.

After a few years, the early morning conference calls and until-midnight-meetings started to eat away at that joy, even more so when a month-long flood wiped out most of our teams' livelihoods. Everyone was feeling the effects of it.

It turned worse after we discovered that, on numerous conference calls, one of our sponsors had been lying about company numbers—info we had since faithfully relayed to our team—and had no interest in coming clean about. It shook my confidence in everyone involved. It was making liars out of us!

A few weeks later, I had enough. The all-star top recruiter for the country noticed that I had a crisis of faith, took me aside before he went on stage to talk to his team, and tried to push me squarely into that round hole: *"If you're OK with seeing thousands of people below you fail and fall away by the wayside, you'll make so much money in this business! Look at everything I have now. You think too much, Chris. Just do exactly what I do. Don't worry about if you can make them successful. Get their money first, so you have your points for the month. Worry about the rest later. Most of them will not succeed anyway!"*

This goes against *everything* ENFJs stand for—integrity, offering the best possible solution, and genuine "leadership."

I'm convinced that only people who already use a product that they swear by daily, who are more driven by helping others

"You can't get much done in life if you only work on the days when you feel good."
—*Jerry West*

than chasing money, who have a vast and compatible network, and who will recruit people with similar values have a chance of finding fulfillment in this career.

The jobs listed below may not offer the level of creative expression or opportunities to inspire and lead that are intrinsic to our ENFJ joy and happiness.

While we may have the skillset for these jobs and often perform them utterly well, we may find these less rewarding.

It's important to consider not just what we're capable of doing but what will bring us the most satisfaction and aligns with our values to ensure a rewarding and fulfilling professional life, as this will contribute to the happiness we experience in our personal life.

If your job is no longer fulfilling or in the list below, it might be worth trying on a new work environment.

✘ Military	✘ Casino Manager
✘ Law Enforcement	✘ Casino Dealer
✘ Factory Supervisor	✘ Cam Model
✘ Power Plant Operator	✘ Tele Evangelist
✘ Chemical Engineer	✘ Stockbroker
✘ Electrical Engineer	✘ Banker
✘ Mechanical Engineer	✘ Teller
✘ Engineering Technician	✘ Accountant
✘ IT Specialist	✘ Auditor
✘ Computer Programmer	✘ Carpenter
✘ Network Marketer	✘ Electrician, Plumber, …

"You're going to pay a price for every bloody thing you do and everything you don't do.
You don't get to choose to not pay a price.
You get to choose which poison you're going to take.
That's it."
—Jordan Peterson

Charting Your Ideal Future (Part 4)

- Which **past careers** have been a clear **mismatch?** Why?

  _____

  _____

  _____

  _____

  _____

  _____

- What lessons or **insights** do you gain from this?

  _____

  _____

  _____

- Which actions will you from now on take to **prevent getting stuck in misaligned work** again?

  _____

  _____

  _____

- **Which careers, categories, and industries do you want to remove?** Use the eraser and afterward write _"I'm becoming more focused on what I really want."_ on the line below.

  _____

*"The best day of your life is the one on which you decide
your life is your own. No apologies or excuses.
No one to lean on, rely on, or blame.
The gift is yours—it is an amazing journey—and
you alone are responsible for the quality of it.
This is the day your life really begins."*
—*Bob Moawad*

— Case Study: Embracing Purpose

From early on, Mark's parents wanted him to have good grades and a well-paid job like they had. So, after earning his business degree, he started working at a consumer goods company.

Though the stable corporate job allowed him financial security, he quickly felt unfulfilled and drained by the rigid, numbers-driven culture. The work environment stifled his desire to collaborate and make a positive impact.

The turning point came when Mark's request to organize a community service day was denied. He realized he was wasting his talents in an environment where profits came before people. During a period of introspection, Mark reflected on past fulfilling experiences where he was mentoring at-risk youth.

He ultimately left the corporate world, moved to another part of town, and became a community organizer. To offset his loss in income, he used his business skills to generate revenue for himself and community members, selling their art, products, and services online.

Though the transition meant taking a pay cut and stepping out of his comfort zone, he could finally use his natural artistic talents, business acumen, and community-building skills to create real change. The deeply meaningful work made the tradeoff worthwhile. Mark is grateful he took control of his professional life and found an environment that energizes him daily.

"Success seems to be connected with action.
Successful people keep moving.
They make mistakes, but they don't quit."
—*Conrad Hilton*

Chapter 5 |
The Perfect Fit

Congratulations! You're ready to pull it all together and choose the best path forward. Here's how it will differ, depending on your current employment and financial situation:

The more financially secure you are, the easier it is to make a more abrupt switch if that's what you want.

If you're still working, you may try on new roles part-time or turn your skills and passions into an online business.

If your finances are in *really* bad shape, restoring that first is essential, as it will **increase your self-confidence.** Luckily, you have plenty of options.

If you're a student, you have the world ahead of you, and with your newfound insights and focus, it's up to you if you want to choose the quickest path to success or the scenic route.

As a fellow ENFJ, I know what you've been going through. I'm right here with you with guidance, tips, and lessons I learned the *really* hard way.

So, know you're not alone.

Now, get your markers ready to highlight the path.

"Pleasure in the job puts perfection in the work."
—Aristotle

You Are Here.

> **Since You're Here!**
>
> Download your FREE bonus material. No matter your path, it will be of tremendous help!
>
> It is available exclusively at **chrisfox.com/enfj-book-bonus**

Highlight your starting point on the map first. You are:

1: RETIRED, FINANCIALLY SECURE.

Money is no longer the most important thing in life, but you crave to do more of what makes your heart sing.

- Choose any of the careers or opportunities that you have shortlisted. You will likely want to pursue the ones **where your presence can make the most significant impact.**

- Also, consider mentoring, volunteering, NGO work, or turning your hobbies and interests into **something lasting and meaningful.**

2: WORKING, FINANCIALLY SECURE.

You have a substantial financial buffer or are willing to sacrifice some income to bring more happiness into your life.

- If you like the company you're working at, find out if **a role better suited to your needs** is available.

"Small opportunities are often the beginning of great enterprises."
—Demosthenes

- Consider **mentoring**, part-time volunteer or NGO work, or turning your hobbies and interests into **something lasting and meaningful.**

- Make a list of your **transferable skills** and **people in your network** who can help you land where you want to be.

- Choose any of the careers or opportunities that you have shortlisted. Depending on your situation, you can either change careers abruptly or try something new on the side, be it **a new career or a business you're passionate about.**

3: WORKING, WANT TO INCREASE INCOME.

Keeping or increasing your current income is essential, but you also want to be *a whole lot happier!*

Your motivation and overall satisfaction with life will increase as you do more work that aligns with your talents, values, and interests. It will also lead to expert-level skills and higher monetary rewards.

- If you like the company you're working at, find out if **a role better suited to your needs** is available.

- If that isn't an option, look at what you want your ideal career to be and **start building the necessary skills** while keeping your current employment.

- Make a list of your **transferable skills** and **people in your network** who can help you land where you want to be.

- Regardless of your job or role, **always make sure to excel.** Wise leaders and ENFJs always look for people who go the extra mile.

"*Crystallize your goals. Make a plan for achieving them and set yourself a deadline.*
Then, with supreme confidence, determination, and disregard for obstacles and other people's criticisms, carry out your plan."
—*Paul J. Meyer*

- If finding a suitable company proves challenging, consider **turning your talents, skills, knowledge, and interests into valuable products or services** until income from those grows big enough to replace your current income.

- Consider **freelancing or starting an online business.** Use your current income to grow your skills and acquire the tools necessary to blow up your side business.

4: IN URGENT NEED TO INCREASE INCOME.

You have lost your main income stream or encountered a series of other mishaps that have led to decision paralysis.

To move forward, you need some urgent wins to **heal your confidence.** The insights from this book will have helped, but it's time to turn them into action. No more slacking, *seriously!*

You're in the worst and best possible place! Worst, as you *need* to make a change *now.* Best, because that urgent need can quickly propel you to where you want to be!

- If you like the company you're working at, see if there's a **higher-paying role** or if they have **a retraining program.**

- Make a list of your **transferable skills** and **people in your network** who can help you land where you want to be.

- Regardless of your job or role, **always make sure to excel.** Wise leaders and ENFJs always look for people who go the extra mile.

- Keeping your ideal career front and center, review the **midway (freelance) jobs or online opportunities** that you have shortlisted, and check out the **complimentary online resources** I have mentioned throughout the book!

"If you don't value your time, neither will others.
Stop giving away your time and talents.
Start charging for it!"
—Kim Garst

- Consider **monetizing your current skills and knowledge** by turning them into digital products or services or doing other online work to pay the bills. You may not like a particular task, but be extremely good at it. Instead of spending the rest of your life doing it, why not perform that daily annoyance one final time? Instead, this time, record a training video and show others how to reach your level of proficiency and turn that utter annoyance into a profit-making machine that will free up your path for something totally different.

- **Picture the end goal in your mind and work your way back to where you are today.** What steps need to happen? What skills do you need to reach the stage just before your ideal career? What comes before that one? And so on.

- If your skill set does not match your ideal career, ensure ample time is left to **build these necessary future skills** while doing whatever is needed to **get back in the blue.**

- **Document it all.** Photos of that worn-out sofa, the mattress on the floor, or the empty house will make for great origin stories **as you rebuild your life and inspire others** on how to do so as well.

- **Surround yourself with people who help you rebuild your confidence**, cheering you on instead of bringing you down. Discuss this with them, or avoid them at all costs!

- **Reality check!** You may need to **check your ego at the door** and make sacrifices to get started, but it's now or never! You know what to do to follow the path that leads to emotional and monetary rewards. *Now, do it.* I would love nothing more than to feature your success story next!

"Greatness isn't achieved in isolation; it's the result of inspiring and impacting others on a grand scale."
—Elon Musk

5: STUDYING, BUILD A LIFE ON YOUR TERMS.

You're already *way* ahead of the rest, knowing the diverse career options that align with your values. So, don't rush. **Try lots of different things**, and **define and own your niche!** Love or hate Elon Musk, but he did the opposite of specializing. He became proficient in many subjects, allowing him to develop innovative ways to improve one industry based on his knowledge of another. If you have the gift of seeing the big picture *and* the minute details, you have greatness waiting inside of you.

- Grow your skills and your **network.** Volunteer, intern, and, by all means, **find mentors** in industries you like.

- Make it a habit to **document** what you're doing as you monetize your newfound skills by freelancing or building online businesses.

- Consider your ideal career and **build passion projects on the side.** You'll see why. It will all click in due time!

"*Trust that still, small voice that says
'This might work, and I'll try it.*'"
—Diane Mariechild

Set Your Destination & Waypoints

Review your answers in the *Charting Your Ideal Future* sections to ensure your path fully aligns with your ENFJ personality:

- Which **themes** or **fields of interest** stand out in your selections? (i.e., coaching, online business, media interests, etc.)

_____   _____

_____   _____

_____   _____

_____   _____

- If you have listed multiple careers in the same field, order them by how few or how many new skills you need to learn.

_____   _____

_____   _____

_____   _____

_____   _____

- **If time and money weren't an issue**, which of these career(s) would you spend your days doing, in order of importance?

_____   _____

_____   _____

_____   _____

Wonderful! My Career Matrix will get you there:

*"We can't become what we need to be
by remaining what we are."*
—*Max De Pree*

HOW TO USE THE CAREER MATRIX

Have a quick peek on the next page to see what it looks like.

First, write down all your careers by order of preference.

Using the same high-to-low (5 to 1) rating system that we used before, rate how well each career corresponds with your *Character Strengths* (STR), *Core Values* (VAL), and *Inner Drives* (DRI) and write the sum total in *Total* (TOT).

In *Top Choices* (TOP), write #1, #2, etc., for the careers with the highest scores. If you have multiple ties, follow your gut—by what you *want* to do, *not* by what you *can* do—or re-evaluate the scores you've assigned earlier.

Next, rate how well your *Current Skills* (CSK) match and how well you want your *Future Skills* (FSK) to match; in other words, how much time and effort you are willing to invest.

This will help you crosscheck if your *Top Choices* are *really* the careers you're after or mere career titles that sound appealing. Without putting the work in, nothing will come of it. If that's the case, either re-evaluate your choices or **commit** right here and now **that you are making it happen.** It's that simple!

This is equally useful if you're transitioning between careers or need to generate income quickly. Look for where you are most skilled and where the FSK has a high number. It will move you closer to your goals.

As a rule, avoid midway careers where your Future Skill interest is smaller than your Current Skill. If you want to package all of your knowledge and sell it online in a book, course, or a set of videos to move to something else, that's fine.

In *Midway Careers* (MID), write #1, #2, etc., for careers or opportunities you have selected along the way to top choices.

*"Progress lies not in enhancing what is,
but in advancing toward what will be."*
—*Khalil Gibran*

Example:

Careers	Character Strengths / STR	Core Values / VAL	Inner Drives / DRI	Total / TOT	Top Choices / TOP	Current Skills / CSK	Future Skills / FSK	Midway Careers / MID
Coaching	5	4	4	13	#1	3	5	#1
Influencer	4	3	5	12	#2	1	5	
Internet Marketing	3	3	3	9	#6	3	4	#2
Web Designer	3	3	2	8	#7	4	2	no
TV Show Host	3	4	3	10	#4	1	3	
Tiktoker	3	3	4	10	#5	1	5	
CEO	3	4	4	11	#3	2	5	

The header also shows: B E S T / E N F J / E V E R

As a *Total* score of 10 was tied, TV Show Host was initially chosen as *Top Choice* #4, and Tiktoker as #5. The score of *Future Skills* tells another story where Tiktoker is rated higher (5) than TV Show Host (3). It could mean there is doubt in our ability or drive ever to become a TV Show Host.

We could double our efforts to become a TV Show Host or switch the *Top Choices* values. Since we start both careers with hardly any skills (1 out of 5), becoming a TikToker first will more likely lead to a TV Host career later.

In *Midway Careers*, Web design is not a good choice. Building the occasional site to pay bills is OK, but the interest is clearly no longer there, as seen in the declining FSK value.

Coaching, combined with Internet Marketing, allows us to monetize quickly as our coaching skills and influence expands.

"If we did all the things we are capable of doing, we would literally astound ourselves."
—*Thomas Edison*

BEST ENFJ EVER CAREER MATRIX

Careers	BEST ENFJ EVER / Character Strengths / STR	Core Values / VAL	Inner Drives / DRI	Total / TOT	Top Choices / TOP	Current Skills / CSK	Future Skills / FSK	Midway Careers / MID

"*Challenge yourself.*
It's the only path which leads to growth."
—*Morgan Freeman*

CHART YOUR PATH

In the box below, **starting from the bottom,** write where you are (your current career). At the top, note where you are going (your Top Choice career). Put the different careers along the way on the map, too. If you know how to draw a mind map, draw the connections between them, and add extra information, such as the training you will take or the skills you need.

where you are going

where you are now ← **start here**

"When I lost my excuses, I found my results."
—*Anonymous*

Obliterating Roadblocks

"What if my career choice doesn't cover my income needs?"

- Can you find an example of someone who *is* making it happen in this field? If so, which excuse is holding you back?

- Which related careers or roles within the industry, or with a similar theme, could be a better financial fit? Get the opinion of someone already in the industry.

- Weigh the pros and cons of sacrificing salary to follow your passion.

- Consider online business opportunities and freelance jobs within your interests that can supplement your passion projects. Added expertise results in higher income.

"How do I choose between my many diverse interests?"

- For each, ask yourself how well you will enjoy it if:

  - You have to do it every day as a job?

  - You have to do it in exchange for money?

- If the answer is "less enjoyable," those are likely hobbies or passions you may want to keep and fund by focusing on other careers.

- Look at the list of people you admire or other authorities in the field for the remaining careers. What do they offer? What will be your service? You don't need to be the most skilled person in the world like they are. Often, people need help from someone just one or a few steps ahead of them. **You are the *ideal* person someone is looking for!**

"To excel at the highest level—or any level, really—you need to believe in yourself, and hands down, one of the highest contributors to my self-confidence has been private coaching."
—Stephen Curry

How Your Brain Tries to Sidetrack You

"I can't find any careers that fully fit my passion!"

- Are you allowing fear (of ridicule, of doing the work, of not being "enough," etc.) to keep you from living a great life?

- Did *anyone else* ever make a career out of that passion? If you're not sure, Google it. Find out how they did. Don't be afraid to follow a similar path, but add your unique flavor! There's a reason why there are multiple brands on the shelves in the supermarket!

- If you spend hours each day on this hobby or passion of yours, document it! You'll become an expert, and experts nearly always make great money!

- There's a case to be made for keeping it your hobby or passion and funding it through any of your other current or future valuable skills. Even traveling or playing games may become a chore for some if it needs to be done daily, for an extended period, just for money!

    - Shortlist the other talents or skills you want to build. When we quickly reach a level of proficiency, our happiness often increases tremendously. These pleasurable tasks could fund your passions.

    - If you still can't find any, then it's more likely that your problem is a **lack of confidence**. Check out the online resources I mention throughout the book to overcome this. Hint: The first step is *taking action!*

"When the winds of change blow, some build walls, and others build windmills."
—Chinese Proverb

And You're on Your Way

- As you're pivoting into better-fitting roles, build or update a *LinkedIn* profile showcasing where you've been and the direction you're heading.

- Search job listings, companies, and roles related to the field.

- When seeking individuals to learn more about an industry, approach them with genuine curiosity. Be clear you're looking to learn, ensuring you don't come across as self-serving.

- Seek advice or mentorship. Insights from those who've already walked this path can be invaluable, offering perspectives you might not have considered.

- Seek out networking events, conferences, and training in the industry. Volunteer, intern, or take short-term gigs to gain experience. Make a plan to obtain the needed skills.

- For those contemplating a more flexible or remote career option, consider exploring online careers. These offer a chance to test the waters without completely shifting from your current job. This path can be advantageous if you hesitate to pursue a new career.

- Before enrolling in courses or training programs, research them thoroughly. Seek testimonials or reviews to ensure the quality and relevancy of the content.

- Avoid too-good-to-be-true programs, especially if your confidence hasn't fully recovered. A whole industry tries to take advantage of people in this situation. Check out the links mentioned in this book for proven and trustworthy resources.

*"Your life doesn't get better by chance.
It gets better by change."*
—*Jim Rohn*

You now know how to more purposefully navigate your career and life as an ENFJ. There is no other personality type like ours where growth plays such an important role. And *growth means change*, so keep this guide close and use it whenever you need to make significant career or life decisions.

🏆 **Your Success Toolkit**

Check out the complementary tools and resources available to expand your skillset at **chrisfox.com/enfj-book-tools**

🥇 **Ongoing Support**

When you feel you would benefit from personalized coaching after reading this book, visit **chrisfox.com/coaching** to explore available programs and services.

*"I can be changed by what happens to me.
But I refuse to be reduced by it."*
—*Maya Angelou*

186

— Case Study: Rising Through Adversity

After being let go from his job as a restaurant manager during the pandemic shutdowns, Miguel took time to reflect on finding more meaningful work aligned with his ENFJ strengths.

He became a life coach, drawing on his natural abilities to motivate and counsel others. Miguel loved helping team members thrive in his previous role and wanted to take this passion further.

Even though he had no formal training, Miguel started by offering free coaching sessions to friends and family to gain experience. Their positive feedback confirmed his talent.

He invested in getting certified as a professional life coach and leveraged his hospitality connections to find speaking opportunities at local events. Within a year of losing his job, he started a flourishing in-person coaching practice. He found the autonomy of self-employment rewarding and was glad he pursued this new path.

Despite the daunting initial career shift, his willingness to take risks and nurture his ENFJ talents led to more significant alignment and fulfillment in life.

"That is the greatest rush;
to see a tangible manifestation of my labors.
To be able to see the impact of my work manifest
in the workspaces, in the shopping malls,
and the places that are providing employment."
—*Brandon Fugal*

Conclusion

As you're ready to start a new chapter in life, I hope you feel empowered, equipped, and energized to align your career with your authentic ENFJ self.

You now have clarity on your strengths, values, and motivations. You know which work environments allow you to shine and which don't. You understand how to evaluate careers for optimal satisfaction and success.

Use this self-knowledge as your compass moving forward. Let it guide you to opportunities where your gifts are valued and make a positive impact. Trust in your strengths, even if others don't always see them. Not everyone will understand your unique wiring. *That's OK. You no longer need their validation.*

Have patience with the process and faith in yourself as you take steps toward greater alignment. **Fulfillment comes not from discovering your purpose but from walking the path more purposefully each day.**

You are the scriptwriter, director, and starring actor in the movie of your life. Surround yourself with a supporting cast that brings out your best performance. The choices you make today write the story of your future.

Make it a masterpiece!

Help other ENFJs get unstuck by recommending this book or sharing your testimonial.

Thank you for being a beacon of change!

Insights

- What has resonated most with you in this book? What insights have you gained? How has this book helped you?

_____

_____

_____

_____

_____

_____

_____

_____

🔔 **Your Feedback Matters**

If you have suggestions for improvement, found errors, or want to share your insights, please do so here:

https://chrisfox.com/enfj-book-feedback

BEST ENFJ EVER

About the Author

Chris Fox is an entrepreneur and coach guiding others toward purpose, prosperity, and happiness.

He has spent over a decade sparking insights that allow people to discover their true potential, empowering them to thrive in relationships, communication, and business.

As a fellow, empathic ENFJ, Chris understands the unique challenges of having wide-ranging passions and honing them into a focused direction.

His life has been punctuated by a series of paranormal experiences since childhood. These mystical journeys have taught him that the observable world is just the tip of the iceberg and that each of us is capable of unimaginable feats.

They have not only ignited his deep fascination with NLP, hypnosis, and the limitless capacities of the subconscious but also fortified his commitment to unlocking human potential. Techniques such as affirmations, alpha-state meditation, brainwave entrainment, and even unconventional approaches like telepathy and remote viewing serve as the building blocks in his quest to elevate personal growth.

He harbors the vision of creating a transformational retreat where these techniques are studied, and individuals can connect to develop their highest potential together.

BEST ENFJ EVER

When he's not helping people in one way or another or immersing himself in a book at a café, you'll find Chris reconnecting with nature, away from the digital world, or indulging in modern Chinese Pop/Rock music—of which he's yet to understand a single lyric.

He resides in Asia, spreading positivity through his coaching practice, social media channels, and his site.

Connect with Chris via his site, **chrisfox.com**, or on social media, search for **chrisfoxdotcom.**

BEST ENFJ EVER

Notes

BEST ENFJ EVER

The Beginning

BEST ENFJ EVER

The Beginning

198

Milton Keynes UK
Ingram Content Group UK Ltd.
UKHW011259221123
433051UK00008B/428

9 789693 892598